CAREERS IN COMPUTER TECHNOLOGY™

CAREERS IN

Digital
Animation

KATHY FURGANG

ROSEN
PUBLISHING

Published in 2014 by The Rosen Publishing Group, Inc.
29 East 21st Street, New York, NY 10010

First Edition

Library of Congress Cataloging-in-Publication Data

Furgang, Kathy.
Careers in digital animation/Kathy Furgang.
    pages cm.—(Careers in computer technology)
Included glossary.
Includes bibliographical references and index.
ISBN 978-1-4488-9591-5 (library binding)
1. Computer animation—Vocational guidance. 2. Computer graphics—Vocational guidance. I. Title.
TR897.7.F87 2014
777'.7023—dc23

2012040223

Manufactured in the United States of America

CPSIA Compliance Information: Batch #S13YA: For further information, contact Rosen Publishing, New York, New York, at 1-800-237-9932.

Contents

To some people, an animated film is not just popular entertainment; it can also be an amazing work of art. The way drawings are brought to life and given their own personal style and energy can amaze even the most critical and serious moviegoer. No longer is animation considered "kid's stuff." It is not confined to movies and Saturday morning television shows. The computer technology of today has seized upon the "look" and techniques of animation and thrust them into every aspect of our media.

As you go through your everyday life, you will come across animation in many forms. The most obvious forms are the cartoons you see on television or the animated films you watch in the movie theater. But computer animation has penetrated into even more areas of our daily lives. Think about the apps you use on your phone or the video games you play on different game systems. Computer games you play on the Internet are examples of the latest in digital animation. You may encounter images as you watch television or movies that you don't realize are examples of digital animation. Even the low-budget commercials you see on TV may use some form of animation. Moving logos in ads or crawling banners on news reports use computer animation as well. And don't forget the special effects in films and television. They are often computer-generated images meant to blend seamlessly into the actual, physically real landscape of the scenes you are watching. If the animation is good enough, you won't even notice where reality ends and digital illusion begins.

Digital animation is not only used to make films but also video games, commercials, simulations, and apps.

Imagine being part of the creative team that designs and produces these different types of animation. There are people working in every part of the computer animation business. Animation has had a long history in visual media, particularly television and film. It continues to spread to other platforms, expand its influence, and amaze the audiences it entertains. Today's animators work faster and with more ease to create effects that were not possible a decade or two ago.

The careers available in computer animation are continuing to expand, just as the field itself is growing. It used to be that only artists were involved in the animation process. Today, it is computer experts who dominate the field and have the greatest employment opportunities. But it's still all about artistry and creativity. Instead of using an ink and brush, today's animator can use computer programs to create dazzling and innovative works of art.

The oldest and most basic kind of animation is traditional 2-D (two-dimensional) animation. This is the creation of the illusion of moving images in a two-dimensional environment. That means that there is no actual depth to the forms. There is only the convincing appearance of it drawn, inked, printed, or painted on a flat surface, such as paper.

This filoscope, invented by a cameraman at the turn of the twentieth century, shows how a series of separate but continuous images can be flipped quickly so that they look like a single image in motion.

You may have experimented with moving images before. A simple flip book is the most rudimentary form of 2-D animation. Suppose you had a stack of index cards held together on one side. Drawing a small figure in the corner of the top page and then drawing the figure in a slightly different position in the same place on the next page, and continuing this process throughout the stack of cards, will result in a good example of a flip book. If you then flip the pages quickly, the image will appear to be moving and changing positions. This is where animation may have had its simplest and most humble beginnings.

CELL ANIMATION

The earliest animators worked without the help of computers. They drew hand-drawn images, each on a single frame with the background drawn in. This method dated back all the way to the early 1900s. Each frame was photographed consecutively and made of many paintings. This was an extremely time-consuming method of creating the illusion of moving images.

Then cell animation was invented. The detailed and time-consuming backgrounds were painted separately, and the characters were drawn on clear pieces of transparent plastic, called celluloid. This was much quicker, and the backgrounds stayed consistent and didn't have to be painted anew behind each successive foreground image. The celluloid frames, or cells, were then placed on top of the background and photographed consecutively. The first cell-animated feature film was Walt Disney's *Snow White and the Seven Dwarfs* in 1937.

Walt Disney's Snow White and the Seven Dwarfs, *released in 1937, was the first feature film to use cell animation in which changing foreground images were overlaid on static backgrounds.*

At the time, this was modern technology. And while it was time consuming to have artists paint each cell that would appear for only a fraction of a second in a feature film, the technique caught on and was used as the primary method of animation for decades. It would take years for a major movie studio to put out a fully animated film using these methods. However, there was a huge consumer demand for the art form. People loved to watch beautifully painted feature-length films

A SCIENTIFIC START

Computer animation got its start in the 1960s in a very scientific way. Research institutes in the United States, often with government funding, were asked to simulate various scientific processes that could not be easily shown with traditional animation. Computer programs were created to help simulate how thick, viscous liquids flow or how shock waves form around an object when it is hit. The mathematical algorithms that the computer programs generated made the work much easier to animate by computer than by traditional animators. These projects helped make computer animation methods easier, faster, and eventually cheaper than the traditional animation methods that had been used for decades. However, it took time for these experimental techniques to be applied more broadly to commercial filmmaking.

with fantastical characters moving through enchanted and enchanting worlds.

ENTER THE COMPUTER

It was not until decades later that the computer began to revolutionize traditional cell animation. The 1978 feature film *Superman* was the first film to use a computer to animate the zooming effect of the Superman logo in the opening title sequence. It would be years before the computer would come to dominate the animation industry, but in the late 1970s and

High-tech animation became common in the animation industry in the 1980s. The Loony Tunes Show, produced by Warner Animation, was a hit around the world and was made primarily with the help of computer animation.

early 1980s, the computer was starting to slowly creep in as a new and innovative tool for animators.

Today, even traditional 2-D animation is created with the help of computers. This is called computer-assisted animation. The computer is an aid to the traditional animation process. It no longer makes sense to pay artists to draw backgrounds, foreground details, and characters over and over again by hand when computer programs can help do the work far more quickly. Instead of using paint, ink, pencil, canvas, paper, or celluloid, the colors, textures, figures, and objects that an artist used to hand-draw can now be created on or scanned into a computer.

One way that traditional animators are greatly assisted by computers is when create the in-between frames that show an object move from one position into another. An artist might create a beginning and ending position of an object or character. The computer program can then use mathematical algorithms to create the in-between poses of the object. This process, called tweening, saves the artist a lot of time drawing every stage of movement between the starting and stopping position. The end result is that the movement will look smooth and seamless, and as fluid as real motion.

There are many careers available in computer animation. As you consider what part of the animation process you would be most suited for, think about the three basic phases of a production. There are jobs available in the preproduction, production, and postproduction phases of a project.

PREPRODUCTION

The preproduction stage of animation is when the project is conceptualized and the look of the film or project is decided upon. This is the stage when the planning should be solidified and the look and feel of the production should be reaching its final stages.

PREPRODUCTION ARTISTS

Preproduction artists are creative and talented artists who work on the earliest stages of a computer animation project. They are trained artists who come up with the look of the characters, interiors, and background landscapes that are being animated. It takes the preproduction artist to turn the director's vision into something that can be visualized, captured, and created digitally so that the other animators further down the production line can make the character come to moving life.

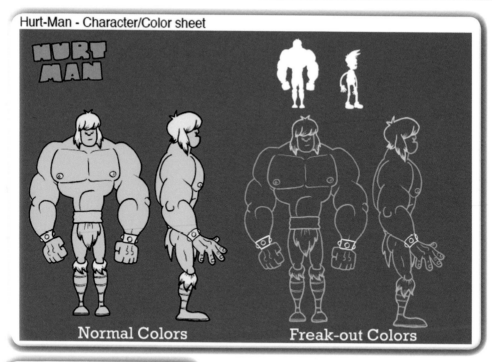

Hurt-Man - Character/Color sheet

HURT MAN

Normal Colors   Freak-out Colors

HEY!

LEAP INTO ACTION!

This character style guide was done by a student at New York University. It shows the character's style and what colors should be used when animating it.

It can take many different attempts and rough drafts of a character before the final version is decided on. And it is not just the main characters who need to be visualized by preproduction artists. Every major and minor character, set design, background, and color choice must be made by preproduction artists in cooperation with the art director and other creative leaders on the project. The decisions that are made at this stage of the production are carried out through each successive step in the process. A preproduction artist must be able to create on screen what a director is visualizing in his or her head. The artist must also be open to criticism and the revision process if his or her initial attempts do not match what the director had in mind.

Even if an artist provides the perfect sketch, one that exactly portrays what an art director has imagined and requested, that does not mean that the sketch will necessarily be approved and the concept will proceed to the next stage. Concepts may change, and storylines may be edited. As a result, some ideas may be revised or dropped entirely along the way.

Preproduction artists may have graduated from art colleges as illustration, painting, or design majors. Animation majors may also be accepted as preproduction artists, but the actual animation that they are trained to do would come much later in the process.

STORYBOARD ARTISTS

Once the look of the characters has been decided upon and approved, it is the job of the storyboard artists to lay out the story, scene by scene and often shot by shot. The storyboard artists might draw the position of each shot by hand, or they may use computer tools to sketch it digitally.

The angle of the camera, the position of the objects and characters in the shot, and the fades of the camera are all things that should be tracked in the storyboarding phase of the project. An animation project is not usually created in

This high school student works on a storyboard as part of a digital animation project at school.

order from beginning to end. Instead, the storyboard will be marked up and divided into pieces so that different teams of animators can work on different parts, all while maintaining a uniform look and feel.

Similar to the work of the preproduction artist, the work of the storyboard artist involves artistic and design training. It also requires thick skin with regard to the number of revisions that could be asked of the artist. Storyboard artists take their direction from the script and the art directors. They must work on tight deadlines to meet the rigorous demands of the production schedule. The schedules are usually extremely tight, and the work must be accurate, with minute attention to detail.

Experienced storyboard artists will be able to include all of the important details and raise questions about anything they notice is left out. The boards can be rough or polished, depending on the direction the artists are given and the time they have to do the job. For computer animation projects, the storyboards are often created with the help of computer graphics programs, but they can also be drawn on paper.

The storyboards help directors and artists visualize and plan ahead of time the way each frame should be shot. This cuts down on errors in the production process later on. The storyboard serves as a roadmap for the entire production as well as a guide to how to arrange the finished pieces sequentially in the later editing stages.

BACKGROUND ARTISTS

The traditional hand-drawn animation work that background artists have been doing for decades is still a valuable skill set in computer animation today. Background specialists are trained artists who may be experienced in painting in a certain style or with a certain palate of colors. Background artists follow the direction laid out in the storyboards. They create scenes that look realistic, whether they are of a suburban living room, a busy city street, a dense forest, or an abandoned warehouse. The backgrounds show everything that is present in the scene except the moving objects or characters. The work of background artists usually starts in the preproduction stage but can continue into the production stage as the details of the story are worked out in animation.

Whether a background artist creates the background scenes on traditional canvas or with the help of computer programs, the work must eventually be put in a digital format so that it can mesh with the rest of the production, including foreground figures and objects. Backgrounds can be scanned into the computer, color levels can be adjusted, textures can be added or changed, and foreground and background elements can be added to or removed from the picture with the click of a mouse.

PRODUCTION

The production stage of the animation process can be complex and involve many animators doing many different jobs simultaneously. This is the stage when the concepts first laid out in the preproduction phase are brought to life. However, there is not just one small, simple step from storyboard to fully animated scene. The animators work in teams to make test shots. They then slowly progress in stages until animations are enhanced and adjusted with further and further detail.

ANIMATORS

There are several levels of animators, depending on one's level of experience and expertise. Animators can work their way up from being an assistant animator to associate animator, and then to master animator.

The production stage begins with the work of the master animator. His or her work serves as a model for the rest of the animators to follow and imitate. Some key shots from the storyboard will be chosen for the master animator to create in animation software programs. This is meant to confirm that the style, layout, and look that were decided upon translate well in actual animated form. Then pencil sketches might be made to ensure that the characters' movements correspond to the way they have been conceived and in a way that is true to their personality and anatomy. These motion sketches will not be highly detailed. They may simply be low-quality images that are meant to be judged on how well they indicate motion and nothing else.

The work of the master animator sets the pace for the other animators. The associate and assistant animators fill in the in-between work in action shots. They also take approved test shots and begin animating individual scenes. The programs they use may initially employ cubes as placeholders for facial features or body parts, but then slowly render the characters and objects in greater detail.

The work that animators do is extremely complicated. They rely upon the help of computer software that creates mathematical algorithms. These are a set of rules followed through calculation or other problem-solving operations. The animation programs can be told where to start and end a span of frames. In this way, they connect the individual frames in such a way as to render them almost like a strip of film, in a seamless progression of sequential moving images from beginning to end.

SOUND TECHNICIANS

When animating a story that features dialogue, the actors' voices are recorded before the characters are actually animated. The actors may be able to see approved pictures of what their characters look like, but the expressivity and emotions of the actors' voices are what give the animator something to play with as he or she animates the scene. The voices of the various characters in a scene are then edited together to mimic the natural flow of back-and-forth conversation.

Technicians work with sound-editing equipment to make several versions of the recordings so that the director can choose the one that works best. This version is then sent to the animators who begin to build the scene visually around the vocal tracks that will be used in the final version of the animated scene.

SOUND EDITORS

The voice work that was done by actors must be edited together in the exact sequence in which it will be heard in a scene.

A WORLDWIDE BUSINESS

While there are certainly many digital animation jobs available in North America, a lot of digital animation is created overseas to keep costs down. The hours needed to dedicate to a project can be very long, and the tasks can be very technical. Especially when schedules are tight, large crews of people in China, Korea, and other countries are hired to perform very technical, demanding, or complex work in the computer animation process. The animation crews overseas take their direction from the creative team that runs the show, usually back in North America.

Actors often record their work in isolation, without the interaction of the other voice actors. An actor may work alone in the studio with just the director and some rough edits of his or her character's movement to look at and react to as he or she delivers the lines. The sound editor then inserts those vocal tracks in with those of the other actors to create a convincing sense of give-and-take conversation within a scene. When the sound editing is finished, it will be impossible to tell that the actors were not in the same room when acting out their lines.

PRODUCTION DESIGNERS

Production designers oversee the work of the animators at all stages of development. As each stage is approved, the production designers can help guide the animators on what needs to be done next. The final background art and coloring are done with a lot of guidance from the production designer, who works closely with and is supervised by the art director.

A production designer oversees several aspects of an animation project, including final background art and coloring.

At each successive stage of the animation process, new layers of detail are added to the scene. The production designer ensures that the work being developed reflects the overall style and design that the art director set out to produce.

POSTPRODUCTION

Many animators work in large teams with a staff of different people overseeing them and helping them do their work. When the animation is finally finished, there is still one last stage to complete before the project comes to an end. This postproduction phase employs many people who specialize in the final stages of the animation process.

EDITORS

Just as in a live-action production, animated projects require editors to choose the best frames and "takes" and edit out anything that now seems unnecessary. With animation, there are far fewer takes to go through because only the best ones make it all the way through the entire rendering process. But the pieces that have been made must be pieced together like a puzzle in the correct order and combined smoothly and seamlessly. This work is done with computer editing programs in which the start and stop of a sequence can be chosen and spliced together with the next sequence that follows consecutively.

The director of Pixar's Ratatouille, *Brad Bird (left), meets with composer Michael Giacchino to record music for the film.*

COMPOSITORS

The job of a compositor is to oversee the consistency of the color and light from frame to frame and from scene to scene with the help of a computer program. Different portions of scenes may have been created by different teams of animators, so the lighting and color used on their computers could be slightly inconsistent from one to the next. Correcting and standardizing light and color can only be done at the end, when the final work is put together.

SOUND MIXERS

What would an animated work be without music? The sound mixer does the job of mixing music over the scenes and having the music tracks start and stop at the right place. The music itself may be chosen by a number of people, including the director and art director. They are hoping to enhance and echo a scene's mood and emotional tone with a complementary piece of music.

Thereʼs a difference between using the computer to help make hand-drawn animation and using the computer to create every bit of every frame of animation from start to finish. After computer-assisted animation became a popular means of producing and expediting hand-drawn work, another digital method was developed that revolutionized the art and made it possible to do all the animation work using only a computer.

ENTERING THE THIRD DIMENSION

Computer-generated animation is different from computer-assisted animation in one big way. Computer-generated animation is performed in a three-dimensional environment, instead of in the flat, two-dimensional environment of traditional animation. To render 3-D animation and create a convincing sense of depth, a computer models the appearance and movements of a physical figure or object that exists in real space.

The ability to add objects to the screen that appear to be three dimensional rather than flat opened a world of possibilities for animation. It made it possible to add animated images to live-action films that featured human actors. These animated figures would look as real and physically alive

In this scene from Jurassic Park, *a computer-generated T-Rex meets up with live-action characters for the first time.*

as the live animals and humans with whom they share the screen. The 1993 film *Jurassic Park* was the first film to use entirely computer-generated characters—dinosaurs—that were convincingly real and integrated flawlessly into scenes with human actors. The dinosaurs in the film showed how computer-generated imagery, or CGI, could be a useful tool in creating special effects that were more convincing than any previous technique in movie-making history.

Just a couple of years later, in 1995, the movie *Toy Story* was the first full-length film made entirely in CGI. The computer

MOVIE MILESTONES

Computer animation has had many milestones that helped move the industry forward. The 2001 film *Final Fantasy: The Spirits Within* was the first feature-length film that used motion capture for all of its character actions. *The Lord of the Rings* series of movies were the first films in which an entirely CGI-created character won an award for a performance. Andy Serkis, who played the character Gollum, won a Critic's Choice Movie Award in a newly created category, Best Digital Acting Performance. In 2004, *Sky Captain and the World of Tomorrow* became the first film in which live actors performed in front of entirely CGI-created backgrounds.

power that is needed to create CGI animation was not available before the 1990s. The technology is improving so quickly that more and more possibilities are open to animators today, and newer and better software programs are becoming available that are easier and faster to use.

WORKING IN THE CGI WORLD

Similar to the way computer-assisted animation crews work, computer-generated animation crews might work in teams to tackle separate parts of a project quickly, each person specializing in one particular chore. In smaller-scale productions, the animators may take on a wide range of tasks. In addition to the careers you have already read about, here are some of the jobs that would be available on a large-scale CGI production.

DIGITAL MATTE PAINTERS

Just as traditional 2-D animations have backgrounds that are painted or drawn by artists, a 3-D production has the same need for background imagery. However, the artist will create these backgrounds in a different way. The use of source photographs, along with 2-D Photoshop images and 3-D animation programs, helps the artists create landscapes that look real and have convincing depth and volume or roundness. Any part of the set painting that characters will interact with must be rendered in 3-D. So if a character's bedroom is the background in a certain scene, it can't simply be a flat backdrop as in hand-drawn cartoons. If the character is going to sit on the bed or open a dresser drawer or close a window, those parts of the background must be 3-D.

The digital matte painter must think about parts of the landscape or background that should be moving. It can be distant cars on a highway, an aquarium with fish circling and making bubbles, or smoke billowing out of a factory stack. The computer program can use mathematical algorithms to create these motions. No longer are backgrounds just static paintings. They are more like real life, in constant motion and flux. They are realistic worlds in which the characters can be placed, interact with each other and the surrounding environment, and act out the story for the viewer.

Digital matte painters have training in fine art as well as computer technology. The computer technology is getting so easy to use that the most talented digital matte painters are not "techies." They are fine artists who can create a wondrous environment that uses exactly the right color palate and textures. Some backgrounds must be historically accurate, so trained artists who can use reference sources as well as the computer to create captivating and convincing animated worlds have an enormous advantage over those with less fine art and art historical training.

MODEL MAKERS

After the style and look of a character have been settled upon by preproduction artists and art directors, it is time for the character to be created. One of the most common ways to make a character is to create a real-life model of it, often out of clay. The purpose of making a 3-D model is to then

Argentinian artist Alberto Couceiro makes numerous models of facial expressions for one of his characters in his animated film TV City.

scan it into the computer so that the character or object can be moved in all directions while still maintaining its three-dimensional plane.

Model makers are trained artists and sculptors who know how parts of the body fit together and move. If the film character is a fish, the model maker must create a clay model that is visually accurate but would take some creative license. For example, areas such as the mouth would not be anatomically correct because the fish character will have to be able to talk. Or its fins may need to gesture much like a human arm would. In the 3-D animation process, there is a fine line between real-life accuracy and artistic license, as well as between the worlds of art and technology.

RIGGERS

After a 3-D model is made, it is not quite ready to be animated yet. The model must go to another person, called a rigger, or character technical director. The rigger prepares the character for animation by setting up a digital skeleton for the character. This is an articulated model, which is built around bones and joints that the creature (whether human, animal, or monster) should have. The joints and skeleton are placed exactly where they would be in the real creature. The computer then records how they move when the arms, legs, shoulder, elbow, wrists, and fingers are manipulated by the rigger. The computer can be set up to limit the movements of these body parts so that they stay within a range that is reasonable and realistic for the character.

The most difficult rigging of all is the subtle movements of the facial muscles that make a character look natural as he or she talks. There are so many muscles involved in the process of speaking and making facial expressions that even master riggers see facial rigging as a huge challenge. But the improvement of rigging software has been making the task easier than ever before.

It used to be that walking was one of the most difficult actions to animate in 3-D. The body uses many more muscles to achieve a walking motion than animators realized. It was a difficult task to make algorithms that made these movements look natural. Many of today's animation software programs come preloaded with algorithms and scripts for body movements associated with walking and other common motions. The work has become so much easier to accomplish, and the guesswork has been taken out of the task. Animators can still write their own scripts for custom movements, but computer programs are even beginning to make specialized movements more accessible to animation artists who aren't programming whizzes.

Rigging, or character technical directing, is, nevertheless, a job for a person comfortable with computer technology and programming. Computer programmers are more likely than fine artists to fill these positions. This is because each character in the production may require special custom-made rigging—and therefore original programming—that standard computer programs can't help an artist achieve.

MOTION CAPTURE TECHNICIANS

Making a model is not the only way to animate a character in three-dimensions. With motion capture technology, a live model can be used to create realistic character movements.

The actor goes to a studio where he or she is fitted with a special suit embedded with dozens of sensors. The sensors are placed on limbs and joints and connected to a computer, which can then detect every movement realistically and accurately.

As the actor walks, jogs, jumps, spins around, or even imitates movements such as flying or diving, the computer digitally records exactly how the body achieved those motions. These digital "motion maps" can then be applied to animated characters in order to make them appear to move in a convincing, anatomically accurate way.

CHARACTER ANIMATORS

Once the character's movements have been captured in the computer either by motion capture or through the model-making and rigging process, the animator is ready to really get down to business making the character come to life. There are many technical aspects to animating in 3-D, from replacing wire frame characters with more fully animated ones, to adding personalized and identifying details to each of the characters, layer upon layer.

The computer does a lot of the difficult and time-consuming work for the animator, helping to fill in movements between key frames that the animator sets up. For example, an animator may choose a key frame in which a character puts a hat on his head. The starting position, ending position, and perhaps one in between are chosen as key frames, and the computer "connects the dots" between these motions. The intervening movements and positions of the

This animated dragon is created on the computer in wire frames.
Movements and colors are then filled in by computer algorithms.

arm and hand will be filled in by the computer. Personalized
and individualized character details are also added by computer. Instead of drawing each strand of individual fur on
an animal's body, the computer adds the fur automatically,
spread out evenly over the character's body, with the desired
thickness and color.

Lighting and color are an important part of 3-D animation,
just as they are essential to 2-D animation. The compositors
do the same kind of checking and adjusting for consistency
to make sure that the lighting and color are consistent from
frame to frame and from scene to scene.

STOP-MOTION ANIMATION

One kind of animation is about as old as the film industry itself. Stop-motion animation typically requires a camera to film only a few frames at a time before stopping and allowing the filmmakers to adjust the figures in the scene to indicate motion and gestures. Filming resumes for another few frames, then stops, and the figures are adjusted again.

There are several different kinds of stop-motion animation. Time-lapse animation involves frame-by-frame stop-and-go filming to reveal the passage of time. These frames can be sped up to show, in mere seconds, the progress of the sun across the sky throughout an entire day, or the blooming and decay of a flower, or the relentless tide of traffic on a busy highway during rush hour. Puppet-based stop-motion animation involves humans moving puppets from frame to frame, and pixilation involves humans moving in tiny intervals from frame to frame and then playing the film in a sped-up fashion. Claymation, or clay animation, involves using clay characters as subjects, with each frame photographed to show the characters' gradual changes in positions.

One of the most famous examples of stop-motion Claymation is the *Wallace and Gromit* series of films, in which clay characters are sculpted and filmed. While the process of Claymation has been around a long time and traditional techniques are still used to make the films, CGI animation is now commonly used for certain elements. Water, fog, or smoke, for example, are created by the computer and combined with the movements of traditional clay characters operating within hand-crafted environments. The viewer may not be able to detect which scenes used the computer and which used traditional methods.

Large productions often have a staff of animators in charge of individual characters. They are in charge of making sure that each character is animated correctly, consistently, and completely from scene to scene. They know everything about that character, its movements, and the way it interacts with its environment and with other characters.

SCRIPT WRITERS

Sometimes 3-D CGI animation programs cannot do everything that the animator wants them to. A script writer is someone who can design special programming script to achieve animated features that typical software cannot. It is a job for a technically accomplished programmer who can write code and solve problems creatively, quickly, and effectively.

RENDERING ARTISTS

An animated feature film can be made at about twenty-four frames per second. That is about 130,000 frames in a single film. Animators must produce a certain number of frames each day or week to stay on schedule. When the work is complete, the frames must be rendered. That is a process done by powerful computers to assemble all of the component parts of the frame into a unified and cohesive whole—the background, the character models, key frames, colors, lighting, and every other element that makes up the finished and complete frame.

SPECIAL EFFECTS ARTISTS

Special effects studios are in charge of making incredible, magical, eye-popping screen moments possible. You may be watching a film that is set in the "real world," with live-action characters doing normal, everyday things. All of a sudden, you may see an explosion, a bridge collapse, or a natural disaster wreaking destruction. Special effects are being put to work in these moments. It is also at work in quieter moments, when filming occurs in spring, for example, but the scene is set in the fall. Computer animation must then change the green leaves to red, orange, and yellow. Or it adds bare branches

In Peter Jackson's live-action series of films The Lord of the Rings, *the character of Gollum was completely computer-generated but based upon the live performance of actor Andy Serkis.*

and snow to create a winter landscape even if the scene is being filmed in high summer. All of these effects—dramatic or subtle—are achieved with the help of digital animation.

Movies such as 1994's *Forrest Gump* were the first to use digital animation to alter the apparent reality of what the viewer was seeing. Inserting Tom Hanks's character within famous news footage and removing the legs of actor Gary Sinise's character were all tricks and illusions created by digital animators.

Other live-action films use digital animation special effects to create elaborate fantasy worlds (*Avatar*, the *Harry Potter* and *Lord of the Rings* series) or historically accurate locales (*Gangs of New York*; *Gladiator*) that are either too difficult or too expensive to create in other ways. Creating a mass of thousands of gladiators, soldiers, or even birds or fish might be done with computer animation rather than with more traditional but cumbersome and expensive special effects methods. Gone are the days when miniature models were meticulously crafted and hung from wire to be filmed in a special effects studio, or elaborate sets were built at enormous cost on a soundstage or in a studio lot. Instead, the computer has become the film industry's most important—and cost effective—special effects tool.

CHAPTER 4

Careers in Video Games, Modeling, and Simulations

Although it is often the first thing that comes to people's mind when they think of digital animation, filmmaking is not the only career option open to those who are interested in the field. There are many other avenues for a digital animator to travel down during his or her career.

Digital animators may work in the video game industry, in advertising, or in the business world. Architecture and medicine are just a few examples of other industries that have benefitted greatly from digital animation. Digital simulations and renderings have helped professionals in these fields conceptualize their abstract ideas; test new technologies, structures, and materials; and experiment with solutions, solve problems, achieve breakthroughs, and visualize that which was previously invisible or nonexistent. Simulations of equipment, vehicles, and scenarios for the military, NASA and aerospace industries, car companies, and weather services and climate studies are other areas that digital animation has both revolutionized and greatly facilitated.

VIDEO GAMES

Animating for video games is a very different task than animating for movies. Playing a video game is an active task, while watching a movie is a passive experience. Getting the user to interact with animated characters on the screen and make them move, speak, and perform actions requires a different set of programming skills, different computer programs, and a different kind of design sense.

A video game is played in a 360-degree field with interconnected landscapes (whether exterior scenes or a series of rooms) that the character or avatar moves through as the story progresses. Video game consoles have a rendering engine that is constantly creating scenes based on where you are directing the character to go and what you are commanding it to do.

This senior concept artist at Epic Games is working on characters for the video game Gears of War 2.

Many video games are rendered in three levels of detail. A low-detail scene is used for wandering quickly through landscapes. Normal-quality scenes are used for action or combat sequences. And the highest quality is used for movielike scenes that relate the story to the viewer with no interaction between the character and his or her environment or other figures. There is simply not enough power yet in video game consoles to render high-quality images as you are moving through landscapes, rooms, and scenes and commanding the characters' actions. However, the video game industry will likely continue to take huge strides forward in terms of how the games look and how they are manipulated by the user.

The skills required of a video game animator include knowledge of the latest animation software. This would include some software that is unique only to video game creation. Other important skills are a good design sense and artistic ability. While the work can be creative at times, it can also be tedious and require attention to many small details. The nature of the work is perfectly suited to someone who is creative, yet technical and detail-oriented.

Video games can be made for handheld devices or for large consoles. The general techniques are the same no matter which device the game is designed for. However, the designers, animators, and technical artists must consider the size of the screens that will deliver the final product. A handheld device does not have the ability to show as much detail as a larger console would. The size of the characters, the speed of the action, and even the print on the screen must be considered when designing for each kind of system.

One computer program that game designers often use is Adobe Flash. Autodesk Maya is also used throughout the film

The computer programs that animators use allow them to control many aspects of the character's movement within a realistic scene.

industry as well as the video game industry. The tool helps with modeling, animation, rendering, and visual effects. Clickteam Multimedia Fusion 2 Developer helps video game developers create environments. MilkShape 3-D is used for importing 3-D models from various file formats. One of the most popular professional tools for developing video games is Unreal Development Kit, or UDK. It enables designers and animators to create realistic scenes within which characters can be inserted.

Video game designers often take their direction from the company that hires them to create the game. For example, Nickelodeon or Cartoon Network might hire a video game design company to create a video game based on the characters from one of its shows. The game company would seek approval for its work at each stage of the creation process to ensure that it was creating the kind of game that the company is expecting.

A professional attitude and clear communication skills are needed in this kind of environment. Similar to the way film crews work, video game makers often divide a project's work load and workflow among several groups of people. Working on a project like that requires good communication skills and a sense of teamwork.

VIDEO GAME IMPROVEMENTS OVER THE YEARS

If you have been playing video games for a long time, you must have noticed the improvement in graphics over the years. Newer software that creates the graphics of animated video games allows many more pixels per inch than previous programs. The pixels are the tiny bits that make up a picture. "Pixel" is short for "picture element." A high ppi, or pixels per inch, will mean that the characters look much more sharp, vivid, and detailed, and can move in smoother and more believable ways.

Another thing that makes new video games look better than ever before is the number of pixels on display screens. No matter how great the quality of a computer graphic is, it can only look as good as the quality of the screen it is being displayed on. A game created with a high ppi must be displayed on a screen with a high number of pixels per inch to look its best.

ADVERTISING

Have you ever gone on the Internet and seen ads in the corner of the screen with dancing characters, zooming cartoons, or slot machine jackpots spitting coins all over your screen? They are also seen during television commercials to display a company's logo or catch the viewer's attention. Many of these animated advertisements are relatively simple to make.

These kinds of short-form animation are called animated GIFs, which stands for "graphics interchange format." The single animation file contains a number of images that are presented in a certain order and can be looped endlessly, creating a flip-book effect on the screen. The GIF can be programmed to stop after a certain point or to continue in an endless loop. GIFs are often used on banners at the top of a Web page or on other Web ads designed to draw your attention. They can be created using the programs Java or Flash.

These simple animations are just the tip of the iceberg regarding the way that animation can be used in advertising. Large advertising firms in New York City may employ artists who specialize in more complex and sophisticated forms of digital animation. Television commercials often use digital animation and have frequently generated groundbreaking ways to present advertising and product content to consumers. Advertising innovation has continued with the advent of new visual platforms, such as the iPad and other Wi-Fi-enabled digital tablets. Whether print-, television-, or Web-based, advertisements can often be considered works of art, and advertising agencies are always welcoming new and talented artists to the field.

Attention to detail and good communication skills are needed for working in the advertising field. It is essential to have a creative and artistic sense in addition to the requisite technical and digital skills. You will also need to master the older analog skills. While the computer animation part of the field is growing fast, the majority of ads will still use traditional film and video techniques.

Adobe Flash is a program that people can use to practice animation techniques. Flash animations are often used in advertising, and they can be relatively simple for people to create on their own. While computer animators working in the advertising field have to seek and receive approval from a client for every creative decision, people just learning the animation techniques have the freedom they need to try new things. Simply getting used to the tools and symbols used in the program can help people decide whether the work truly suits and interests them.

ANIMATION IN OTHER INDUSTRIES

Computer animation has a creative and innovative appeal, so why is it so important in industries that don't initially seem to be so creative, such as medicine, the military, architecture, meteorology and climate, and the aerospace and automotive industries? First of all, these industries actually do depend upon abundant creativity and imagination for their innovations, designs, operations, and planning. There is a need for accurate recreations, simulations, models, and realistic designs in all of these industries to help people plan new projects and understand new concepts.

For example, a new car design must be created in the planning stage before it can be reviewed, approved, and then built and sold. There may be countless changes to the design of the car along the way. This is where the computer comes in. Three-dimensional models of the car can be made, and the design can be examined at all angles. The aerodynamics and exterior and interior design features can be revised and adjusted on the computer, and approval can be obtained before expensive prototypes are made of real materials.

Computer animation allows designers to see what a model would look like from various angles. It allows changes to be made easily without incurring additional production expenses.

Auto industry computer simulations were first developed in the late 1950s by General Motors and IBM. These first animation and modeling systems were very limited, but they allowed models to be created digitally from scanned pencil-and-paper sketches. These rudimentary programs were replaced by the computer-assisted design (CAD) programs that were developed and used years later. These systems were developed specifically with car design in mind. Engineers could now design the car down to its last nut or bolt, using computer graphics to aid in the process. Computer animations are also a good way for executives to communicate their ideas to employees about new projects and even to investors to explain exciting new endeavors the company may be exploring.

The military uses computer animation to simulate important military operations so that everyone involved can anticipate some of the variables they may encounter and plot what should be happening and where each person should be situated during each stage of the mission. It also allows soldiers to test and improve their split-second decision-making skills, which can have life-or-death implications.

Architectural firms may also use computer animation to illustrate the building stages of a construction process and analyze the strength and integrity of structures and building materials. Instead of simply showing what the finished product will look like, the animations also help planners estimate how long each phase might take, what materials will be necessary in what quantity, and what the costs of materials and labor are likely to be.

The design and building of a new railway system, bridge, or other expensive public infrastructure or commercial development endeavor can be computer animated to show investors

Computer-aided design can help architects demonstrate what an interior or exterior of a building will look like. This helps communicate ideas to builders, interior designers, and clients.

what the project would entail, how it would impact the landscape or the environment, what the finished product would look like, how it would operate, and how well it would hold up under various kinds of stresses. This gives investors a good idea of whether they would like to take part in the financing of the program.

New medical procedures can be animated on computers for research and training purposes. Digital animation is also useful for educating the general public by showing what can happen inside the body as different diseases run their course or harmful physical and dietary habits take their toll. Animations can show patients why different surgeries may be needed, how particular surgical options differ, and how different medications work to fight the symptoms or sources of illness. These computer animations are sometimes used even on television commercials to advertise medications.

Animators working for the military or private industry may need additional training in medicine, architecture, or aerospace engineering. A person working to animate a technical and specialized military or industrial process or product must follow careful instructions. Errors can be very costly, in terms of both money and lives. Military and industrial animations must be technically accurate above all else. Design, color, lighting, and other aesthetic considerations may take a back seat to the technical accuracy of the process being animated. In some cases, calculations provided by engineers and other scientists are used to help guarantee the accuracy of the animations.

CHAPTER 5

Preparing for a Career in Digital Animation

The world of digital animation provides a wealth of opportunity for a young person who wishes to prepare early for a career in the field. Even if you already have a college and career path laid out before you, it is wise to get hands-on experience in the field as soon as possible. This way you can test out whether or not you really enjoy the work and feel suited to do it. You should also begin to give some thought to what area of the animation field you would like to specialize in, whether it be film, television, video game graphics, advertising, or technical industries.

HIGH SCHOOL COURSES

The classes you take in high school can do more than just help you get your diploma. If they are carefully chosen, especially in your junior and senior year when you have a wider range of electives, there are things you can do to help prepare for a career. Most schools have electives in computer science and art. Both of these areas of study can help you test your abilities and aptitude for digital animation.

Standard drawing classes can help you determine if you have the basic talent necessary for any animator to possess, whether working in hand-drawn or digital animation. Drawing skills are especially important for the preproduction artists and designers who work on animated film projects.

Model making—whether in the analog or digital realm—takes years of artistic training. Classes in art and sculpture can help some people prepare for character creation and modeling work in the field of hand-drawn, digital, stop-motion, and clay-based animation.

Drawing skills might also involve technical drawing. Many schools offer courses in architectural drafting and technical drawing. These are courses in which you might convert an idea, such as a building design, into a physical form, such as a blueprint or other plan. Computer programs such as CorelDraw can help students create renderings that show perspective, scale, and three-dimensional views. The programs can help create objects shown from the top and from any side. These skills can be useful for someone interested in creating technical animations for industries such as architecture or automotive design.

If your high school does not have classes such as these, you can look online for courses offered at community centers or local community and trade or technical colleges that accept high school students.

CHOOSING A COLLEGE

Choosing a college can be a daunting task for anyone, but knowing what you want to focus on can help make the task just a little bit easier. Researching schools that offer majors in animation might be the most direct route to take. Looking into art schools may be the first step to take. Some smaller art programs may not offer computer animation majors. So it helps to do as much research about each prospective college's offerings and programs as possible before choosing among them and committing to attend one.

Once you have found some colleges that feature the programs you are looking for, make sure that you look into the specifics of what they offer and what equipment and materials purchases might be required of students. Some schools may require students to work on school computers to ensure that everyone is using the same hardware and software. Other schools may require that students purchase all of the necessary hardware and software themselves. This could be a deciding factor for some families who have a limited budget and can't afford a lot of additional expenses beyond tuition and room and board.

Keep in mind that if you become a computer animation major, you may be required to take some courses in art history and the fine arts, such as drawing or painting. You must be willing to fulfill the requirements of the major that you choose, even if you intend to focus on just one specific area of

Three-D animation programs can help users create realistic digital worlds, such as rooms with furniture into which characters can be placed.

the art world and even if your interest is more in the programming and technical end of digital animation.

Film schools are also worth considering if you hope to begin building a career in digital animation. Many film schools now offer digital animation majors, but you will probably also have to take film history and live-action and documentary filmmaking classes. This will not be time wasted, as the best animators are those with the richest sense of art and film history and the greatest range of experience across art mediums, such as drawing, painting, and traditional filmmaking.

Instead of pursuing a career in digital animation through an art major or film school, you can partake of any animation classes offered by community colleges and trade and technical schools in your area. These schools often specialize in computer science and other digital and electronic technologies. The animation programs at these schools would probably emphasize technology over art and aesthetics. Programming, algorithms, and problem solving will probably be emphasized over the creation of characters, stories, and an overall aesthetic vision.

If you are unsure about which kind of computer animation program of study you are interested in pursuing, read the course descriptions offered by each of your prospective schools. The course descriptions should be able to help you decide whether the courses sound interesting and whether they focus on aspects of the field that appeal to you. Also try to find out what software and animation programs are used and taught in the classes. Some schools use state-of-the-art programs, while other schools may be years behind the current technologies. In a field that changes so quickly, it is important to find out if you really are getting an education that will prepare you for a career in the field of your choice.

TECHNICAL AND TRADE SCHOOLS

After researching college programs, you may find that the four-year college path is not for you. There may be a lot of prerequisites and major requirements that do not relate directly to the aspect of digital animation upon which you wish to focus. The degree may also take too long to obtain and at too high a cost. For someone who just wants to learn the trade in an immediate, hands-on way, technical and trade schools, community colleges, and certificate programs may be the way to go.

Another reason that technical schools are a good idea is that computer programs for animation change so quickly that much of what you have learned may be obsolete by the time you graduate from a four-year school. Technical schools typically offer classes without requiring students to earn a degree. That means you may not have to take all of the required courses that a four-year college demands, and the courses you do take can all be focused upon your specific field of interest.

INTERNSHIPS

An internship is a job experience, usually unpaid or very low-paying, that is offered to a young person who is still a student or just setting out on a career. Oftentimes, the hands-on professional experience and school credit are the only official compensation for the work. Many colleges work with businesses to offer internships to students, but some high school students may be able to seek out such opportunities as well.

ARE YOU A MATH TYPE?

When considering what kind of digital animation you are most suited for, think about what kind of person you are. Do you think of yourself as a techie whom everyone else goes to for help with their computers, software, electronics, and digital devices? Are you a problem solver and an analytical thinker? You might be best suited for the technical end of digital animation. There can be a lot of math, measurements, algorithms, programming, and small, technical details involved in the work. This is especially true if the animations are meant for aeronautical, automotive, architectural, or medical industries. Only those students with meticulous, mathematical minds should attempt the technical end of digital animation.

A school guidance counselor might be able to help you set up an internship with a local advertising company, television station, film studio, or other business that uses computer animation in some capacity.

The work that a high school intern might be asked to do will not likely be the work of a junior animator or someone who works full-time in the field. It would more likely be office work such as filing, data entry, answering phones, photocopying, and letter writing. The point of an internship is not to become fully trained in a field, but to get an overview of a certain business and learn what it might be like to have a job in that industry.

The networking opportunities offered by internships are among the most valuable benefits of the work experience. An

These programmers are working on a game development competition. Networking and meeting other people in the animation field can help people develop their careers.

intern will be introduced to people with different job titles who work on every aspect of the business. These people can explain what they do, how they do it, what they studied to get there, and if they like it. They can also provide references and letters of recommendation for you when applying to college or for paying jobs during and after college.

The school credits you earn during an internship can often be applied to any art, business, or technology requirements you must satisfy before graduating. Very often, interns meet with a contact person at their school, such as an academic adviser, during and after the internship to offer status reports on the work being done and the valuable lessons being learned. The adviser can help answer your questions and help you parlay your work experience into greater success in the college admissions and career-building processes that will follow the internship.

Not only do high school internships help students decide whether or not they actually enjoy and have an aptitude for a certain field of study, they also greatly enhance a college application and résumé. An internship shows that the student has already identified his or her interests and has taken the initiative to seek and obtain professional experience in that field. Internships can help students get accepted into their college of choice. The supervisor of the internship experience can also be a great person to ask for a college admissions letter of recommendation.

Be aware, however, that internships are not always easy to find for high school students. Very often, the high schooler must take the initiative and ask around at places that interest him or her. Experiences like these can be the most valuable of all because they are customized to the student's interests and needs.

JOB EXPERIENCE

Not every high school student goes to college, community college, or technical school after graduation. Some move directly into the workforce. Someone who is interested in the field of digital animation may wish to go right into the field and start working immediately. This is easier said than done, however. While on-the-job training in animation programs is possible, the chance that a recent high school graduate would land a job in animation with no experience is slim.

The opportunity to move to the animation department from another department within a company is slightly more likely. Suppose you work for an advertising company in the human resources or public relations departments in charge of employee benefits, company finances, and customer relationships. The company may also have a department that designs animation for use in short advertisements. If an entry-level job opens in that department, you might wish to interview for it.

Companies often prefer to hire from within because the person being hired is already a known quantity. People will know you and your work habits, and they will know that you can be trusted to learn a new program or meet deadlines well. From there, you can be on your way to learning the ins and outs of the computer animation programs and handling many aspects of the animated production process.

LEARN THE PROGRAMS

Sometimes all that a person needs to do to start working in the animation field is show that he or she knows how to use the necessary computer programs. Maya, Flash, and other programs can be learned at home or by taking computer courses and tutorials in your community. Using tutorials that are available online or come with the programs and obtaining the user manuals from the library, a bookstore, or online can be all the start you need. If you have an aptitude for this kind of work, you will soon teach yourself much of what you need to know and achieve mastery over all the programs relevant to digital animation.

Animators must keep up on the latest programs. This animator uses Autodesk Maya, Autodesk Mudbox, and Autodesk Smoke.

Adobe Flash offers tutorials that can help you design and animate your own characters. You are walked through the entire process, starting with conceptualizing a character either by drawing it with Flash tools or scanning a hand drawing. Another part of the process involves converting objects to symbols and assigning unique behaviors to the objects. Adding special and unique effects to the objects, editing their motions, and storing and archiving the animation files are skills that a motivated person can learn on his or her own by viewing tutorials or following the step-by-step instructions in software manuals.

ARE YOU THE ARTISTIC TYPE?

As you think about what kind of animation job you might be most suited for, consider what makes you happy. When you see digital animation, what amazes you most about it? Are you dazzled by the sheer beauty of the work and the artistic accomplishment? Or are you more fascinated by the way in which programming a series of 1s and 0s can create the convincing illusion of both real and fantastical worlds and creatures? If it's the artistic rather than the mathematical and technological feats that most inspire you, you will probably most enjoy the artistic end of digital animation, such as the preproduction work that results in character and landscape creation and the shading, coloring, and lighting of scenes throughout the production process.

Working on your own projects and building up a body of work can develop and expand your creativity and help you discover what particular aspects of digital animation you like best and are most skilled in. It will also allow you to begin developing an impressive portfolio that can be shown to potential employers and college admissions officers.

MAKE A PORTFOLIO

Whether you are trying to get into a college, secure an internship, or land a job in the field of digital animation, a portfolio can help showcase your technical skills and abilities and your artistic flair. Digital portfolios are meant to highlight work that is either difficult or impossible to print and display in a physical folder of static 2D work. A digital portfolio can be a collection of animations stored on DVD, in an MP3 file, or at an online location. It allows someone to view examples of your work that demonstrate your varied technical abilities and stylistic range.

Animated GIFs (short animations made with Flash and Java) can help show a prospective college acceptance board or employer what you are capable of. Remember to include only examples that you have worked on yourself, either solo or as part of a team. If the example is drawn from a group project, be truthful about exactly what your role was and what part of the work is yours. A portfolio must be an honest account of your work. It can be periodically updated to include new projects as you finish them. Older pieces may be removed if you feel that they no longer accurately represent your skill level or range, your artistic vision, or the kind of work that you would like to do in the future.

CHAPTER 6

Staying on Top: Networking and Lifelong Learning

One thing that you can count on in the digital animation industry is that it will never stop changing and evolving into something new and forward-looking. Just look back ten years ago. The animation world did not look remotely like it does today. Ten years from now, the industry and its products will be rendered similarly unrecognizable by revolutionary technological and

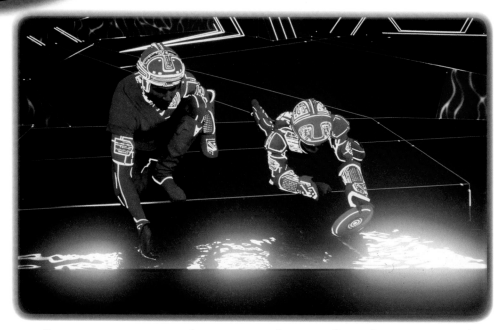

Tron was innovative and inventive at the time of its release in 1982, but today it looks quaint and rudimentary. The computer-animated films that currently dazzle and amaze will also be overtaken by even more awe-inspiring technological advances and capabilities.

artistic innovation. The groundbreaking and paradigm-shifting innovations ushered in by the movie *Tron* back in 1982 look antiquated and rudimentary today. Amateur animation enthusiasts using store-bought software and a home computer can easily surpass the special effects that made *Tron* such a mind-blowing experience for contemporary film audiences.

That's why it is important to keep looking ahead to the future of animation. Even the best animators in the business must continually familiarize themselves with the latest technologies, innovations, hardware, and software. Most technological developments are evolutionary and incremental. For example, animators may learn the quirks of new versions of old and familiar software, but the nature of the work and the tools they use don't change dramatically. Until they do. Once in a while, an innovation is introduced that completely changes the way work is produced. It quickly becomes the new industry standard, and those who don't learn and adopt it are in danger of being left behind.

STAY INFORMED

Reading film industry and computer technology periodicals and newsletters can help you stay on top of the latest developments in the field. You don't need to read these every week, or even every month. But once in a while, check out the film or technology section of a newspaper or magazine to see what new ideas are being talked about. Visit Web sites like Wired.com and AnimationInsider.net.

The release of each new animated or CGI-heavy live-action film is usually accompanied by dozens of articles and television segments on the latest techniques and programs

Keeping up on current technology and programming and experimenting with the latest programs is essential for sustaining and advancing a lifelong career in animation.

that artists and animators used while working on the project. Any time a movie or other animated product is the "first" to accomplish something, take note of how the new effects were achieved and what tools were used. The better informed you are, the better you will understand how any industry innovations may affect you and the work you are doing now and will do in the future.

The release of new products can also help keep animators on top of their game. New software tends to make work faster, easier, more efficient, and more visually impressive than before. Comparing the features of the new software with what you are already using can help you learn whether the

MAKE YOUR OWN PROJECT

Think of an idea that you would like to focus on, whether it be to create a short film, an advertisement, or an animated logo. Plan the project out first and then revise it accordingly as you begin working on it. Troubleshoot any unexpected glitches or problems. Decide ahead of time what software you will need to use and whether you will need to create models or use your own drawings. Decide on whether you will use storyboards and what kind of editing you will do once you have finished the animation process. When you are done, present your project to someone, whether it be friends, family, or an art or technology teacher at school. If you are pleased with the project, include it in the digital portfolio you will share with college admissions officers and prospective employers.

new capabilities and tools justify the expense. Read product reviews and ask around. It might be wise to wait a while before updating or adopting the new hardware or software until you collect a range of users' opinions and feedback.

SHARPEN YOUR SKILLS

They say no one can teach someone else how to be creative. That may be true, but someone can be taught art and computer skills. And sometimes simply doing the work—through trial and error—is the best teacher of all. Keep practicing your drawing, painting, storyboarding, and creating of models. Continuous, lifelong practice will both sharpen your skills and encourage a steady flow of creative ideas and experiments. You can also work with friends to make your projects more interesting.

MAKE CONNECTIONS

As any successful businessperson can tell you, it helps to make connections. The people you meet through school and work can be a great help in many ways. Your former teachers, professors, bosses, and coworkers can notify you of job openings in the industry, provide references to prospective employers, and write you letters of recommendation. Maintain good

Receiving help, advice, and recommendations from teachers and mentors can help young animators get a start on their careers.

relationships with everyone you work and study with. You can help each other with career advancement and the lifelong learning that will keep you on top of your field. People with mutual respect for each other and each other's work can have good professional relationships that last an entire career and are mutually rewarding and enriching.

Once a project is finished, the animator must find another project to work on. It is rare for an animator to have a permanent job working for the same company for many years. Each movie, television, or advertising project is staffed for the duration of the production, and the animators will then move on when the project is done. That's why having solid connections and an extensive social network that you can count on is a good way to keep your career going.

Your reputation is also an important part of building good connections. When people get to know your work and your work ethic, you establish the kind of trustworthiness, integrity, and reliability that will get you hired for projects and further your career.

Glossary

animated GIF Bitmap image format, called graphics interchange format; a moving image usually made for a Web page.

architectural drafting Technical drawing of a building, usually done by an architect.

articulated model Three-dimensional model connected by flexible joints for posing.

celluloid A tough kind of plastic that was used in the past to make photographic film and other products; the film used to make movies.

Claymation A method of animation in which clay figures are filmed using stop-motion film techniques.

compositor The person working on an animated film who oversees consistency of light and color from frame to frame and scene-to-scene.

computer-assisted animation Method of animation that uses computer techniques in conjunction with traditional animation methods.

computer-generated animation Method of animation that uses imagery that has been entirely created on and manipulated by a computer.

continuity Consistency in a film or other project from frame to frame or from scene to scene so that, for example, a character wearing eyeglasses in one part of a scene continues to wear them in another part of the scene that may have been animated or filmed at a different time.

key frame Frame in an animated film that has been designated as particularly important within a scene or sequence.

postproduction Work done on a film project after the filming or animation has been completed.

preproduction Work done on a film project before the filming or animation has been completed.

production Work done on a film project that involves filming or animating the story as set out in the script and storyboard.

rendering The process of generating an image from a model by using computer programs.

rigging The process by which a 3-D character is modeled for animation.

scanning Transforming an image into a digital copy that can then be manipulated by computer, displayed, and stored and sent electronically.

storyboard A sequence of drawings representing the shots planned for a film or animated production; a sort of visual script or road map to a film.

three-dimensional Describing graphics that give the appearance of an object being on three planes, or a coordinate system with three axes.

tweening Process of generating the intermediate frames between two key frames, usually performed by a computer. For example, the first key frame might be an animated character hearing a doorbell ring. The second one might be that character opening the front door. The computer would animate all the frames in between, in which the character is walking to the front door.

two-dimensional Describing images seen on a flat plane, such as photographs, drawings, paintings, and in traditional films and television.

For More Information

AnimAction, Inc.
22287 Mulholland Highway, Number 99
Calabasas, CA 91302
(818) 222-4690
Web site: http://www.animaction.com
AnimAction provides workshops for teens to collaborate on
animation projects and holds screenings of these projects
in schools and communities.

Canada Summer Jobs
Service Canada
Canada Enquiry Centre
Ottawa, ON K1A OJ9
Canada
(800) 935-5555
Web site: http://www.servicecanada.gc.ca/eng/epb/yi/yep
/programs/scpp.shtml
Canada Summer Jobs is a government of Canada initiative
that provides funding to help employers create summer job opportunities for students. It is designed to
focus on local priorities, while helping both students
and their communities. Canada Summer Jobs provides
work experiences for students and supports organiza-
tions, including those that provide important community
services.

Discovery Internships
134 West 26th Street, Suite 1200

New York, NY 10001

(212) 367-5695

Web site: http://www.highschoolinternships.com
/high-school

This group provides customized internship programs for
high school students.

DoSomething.org

19 West 21st Street, 8th Floor

New York, NY 10010

(212) 254-2390

Web site: http://www.dosomething.org

This organization is dedicated to social change. It accepts
interns who are committed self-starters, including tech
wizard interns.

Dream Careers

2221 Broadway Street

Redwood City, CA 94063

(800) 251-2933

Web site: http://www.summerinternships.com

Dream Careers provides summer internship opportunities in
the film industry for college students.

Junior Achievement

One Education Way

Colorado Springs, CO 80906

(719) 540-8000

Web site: http://www.ja.org

This volunteer-based group is dedicated to educating young
people about business and economics education.

Lucasfilm Animation
P.O. Box 29901
San Francisco, CA 94129
Web site: http://www.lucasfilm.com/divisions/animation
Founded in 2003, Lucasfilm Animation is a digital animation
    studio launched to produce *Star Wars: The Clone Wars,*
    a computer-generated, weekly animated series. In addi-
    tion to continuing work on *Star Wars: The Clone Wars* and
    developing a second *Star Wars* animated series, the studio
    is also focusing efforts on feature film animation and
    other new intellectual properties.

Media Job Search Canada
1403 Royal York Road, Suite 608
Toronto, ON M9P 0A1
Canada
(416) 651-5111
Web site: http://www.mediajobsearchcanada.com
This is a job search service for Canadians interested in jobs
    in the media.

Nickelodeon Animation Studio
231 West Olive Avenue
Burbank, CA 91502
(818) 736-3000
Web site: http://nickanimationcareers.com
The Nickelodeon Animation Studio offers cutting-edge
    animation technology, allowing artists to combine
    traditional cell animation with the newest digital technol-
    ogies, including CG, 3-D, and motion capture.

Walt Disney Animation Studios
500 South Buena Vista Street
Burbank, CA 91521-4850
Web site: http://www.disneyanimation.com
Walt Disney Animation Studios brings imagination to life
through traditional and computer-animated films. Its
crew is filled with diverse talent from all around the
globe whose passion is to create beautiful and timeless
films through the art of storytelling, the magic of animation, and the science of cutting-edge technology.

Walter Lanz Digital Animation Studio
UCLA School of Theater, Film, and Television
102 East Melnitz Hall, Box 951622
Los Angeles, CA 90095-1622
(310) 825-5761
Web site: http://www.tft.ucla.edu/the-walter-lantz-digital
-animation-studio
In 2000, the UCLA Animation Workshop received an award
of $500,000 from the Walter Lantz Foundation to build a
studio and state-of-the-art student workspace to continue
the workshop's development of digital animation.

WEB SITES

Due to the changing nature of Internet links, Rosen Publishing
has developed an online list of Web sites related to the subject
of this book. This site is updated regularly. Please use this link
to access the list:

http://www.rosenlinks.com/CICT/DiAn

For Further Reading

Cabrera, Cheryl. *Reel Success: Creating Demo Reels and Animation Portfolios.* New York, NY: Focal Press, 2013.

Cantor, Jeremy. *Secrets of CG Short Filmmakers.* New York, NY: Course Technology, 2013.

Duggan, Michael. *2D Game Building for Teens.* Boston, MA: Course Technology PTR, 2011.

Ham, Ethan. *The Building Blocks of Game Design.* New York, NY: Routledge, 2013.

Keller, Debra. *Creating 2D Animation with Adobe CS6.* New York, NY: Delmar Cengage Learning, 2013.

Kerlow, Isaac. *The Art of 3D Computer Animation and Effects.* Hoboken, NJ: Wiley, 2009.

O'Hailey, Tina. *Rig It Right! Maya Animation Rigging Concepts.* New York, NY: Focal Press, 2013.

Sethi, Maneesh. *3D Game Programming for Teens.* Boston, MA: Course Technology PTR, 2009.

Vaughan, William. *Digital Modeling.* Berkeley, CA: New Rider's Press, 2012.

Williams, Richard. *The Animator's Survival Kit, Expanded Edition: A Manual of Methods, Principles, and Formulas for Classical, Computer, Games, Stop Motion, and Internet Animators.* London, England: Faber & Faber, 2009.

Wyatt, Andy. *The Complete Digital Animation Course: Principles, Practices, and Techniques: A Practical Guide for Aspiring Animators.* Hauppauge, NY: Barron's Educational Series, 2010.

ACM Siggraph Education Committee. "Introduction
    to Computer Animation." Retrieved August 2012
    (http://old.siggraph.org/education).
All Computer Schools. "Looking for a Program at All
    Computer Schools?" Retrieved August 2012 (http://www
    .all-computer-schools.com/computer-careers/animation
    /careers-computer-animationv).
Barton, Matt. *Honoring the Code: Conversations with Great Game
    Designers.* Oxfordshire, England: AK Peters, 2013.
Campbell, Nicole. "Careers in the Computer Industry."
    eHow. Retrieved August 2012 (http://www.ehow.com
    /about_5398557_careers-computer-industry.html).
Cinnamon, Ian. *Programming Video Games for the Evil Genius.*
    New York, NY: McGraw-Hill/TAB Electronics, 2008.
CreativeSkillSet.org. "Understanding Animation." Retrieved
    August 2012 (http://www.creativeskillset.org/animation
    /careers/article_3768_1.asp).
Crosby, Tim. "How Becoming a Video Game Designer
    Works." HowStuffWorks.com. Retrieved August 2012
    (http://electronics.howstuffworks.com/video-game
    -designer.htm).
Dawson, Nick. "A Short History of Stop Motion." Focus
    Features, February 6, 2009. Retrieved August 2012
    (http://focusfeatures.com/article/a_short_history
    _of_stop_motion).
Entertainment Magazine. "Wallace & Gromit: About the
    Production: The Long and Short of It." 2004. Retrieved

August 2012 (http://emol.org/film/archives /wallacegromit/production.html).

Georgenes, Chris. "Designing and Animating Characters in Flash—Part 1: Drawing Tools and Symbols." Adobe.com. Retrieved August 2012 (http://www.adobe.com/devnet /flash/articles/design_character_pt1.html).

Goldsmith, Alexis. *Learning CSS3 Animations & Transitions: A Hands-on Guide to Animating in CSS3 with Transforms, Transitions, Keyframes, and JavaScripts.* New York, NY: Addison-Wessley, 2012.

Hartman, Dennis. "Types of Computer Animation." eHow. com. Retrieved August 2012 (http://www.ehow.com/ about_5256092_types-computer-animation.html).

InternalDrive.com. "Software Used in Game Design & Modding Camps." Retrieved August 2012 (http://www.internaldrive .com/courses-programs/tech-products-used-at-our-summer -computer-camps/id-video-game-camp-partners-summer -computer-camp-technology-partners).

Internships.com. "IT/Computer Technology Internships." Retrieved August 2012 (http://www.internships.com /intern/it).

Kichura, Venice. "What Is Technical Drawing?" eHow.com. Retrieved August 2012 (http://www.ehow.com /about_5056870_technical-drawing.html).

Lealos, Shawn S. "From Zoetrope to Pixar: Animation Through the Years." Bright Hub, June 9, 2011. Retrieved August 2012 (http://www.brighthub.com/multimedia /video/articles/59159.aspx).

Naillon, Buffy. "Traditional vs. Computer Animation." eHow. com. Retrieved August 2012 (http://www.ehow.com /facts_5765261_traditional-vs_-computer-animation.html).

Naillon, Buffy. "2D Animation vs. 3D Animation." eHow.
com. Retrieved August 2012 (http://www.ehow.com
/facts_5834100_2d-animation-vs_-3d-animation.html).

Ohio State University. "A Critical History of Computer
Graphics and Animation." Ohio State University.
Retrieved August 2012 (http://design.osu.edu/carlson
/history/lesson2.html).

Omega. "Timeline CGI History." Retrieved August 2012
(http://omega.cs.iit.edu/~hycdani/projects
/computersandmovies/timeline.htm).

Roos, Dave. "How Computer Animation Works."
HowStuffWorks.com. Retrieved August 2012 (http://
entertainment.howstuffworks.com/computer
-animation1.htm).

Sanders, Adrien-Luc. "Animating for Video Games vs.
Animating for Movies." About.com. Retrieved August
2012 (http://animation.about.com/od
/videogameanimation/a/gamesvsmovies.htm).

Scaramozzino, Michael. *Creating a 3D Animated CGI Short: The
Making of the Autiton Archives Fault Effect.* Burlington, MA:
Jones & Bartlett, 2010.

Slick, Justin. "What Is Rigging?" About.com. Retrieved
August 2012 (http://3d.about.com/od/Creating-3D
-The-CG-Pipeline/a/What-Is-Rigging.htm).

TopTenReviews.com. "2012 Best 3D Animation Software
Comparisons and Reviews." Retrieved August 2012
(http://3d-animation-software-review.toptenreviews.com).

wiseGEEK. "What Does a Storyboard Artist Do?" Retrieved
August 2012 (http://www.wisegeekedu.com/what-does
-a-storyboard-artist-do.htm).

Index

ABOUT THE AUTHOR

Kathy Furgang has written numerous books for Rosen Publishing about the Internet, computers, and the economy. She lives in upstate New York with her husband and two sons.

PHOTO CREDITS

Cover (background), p. 1 © iStockphoto.com/Andrey Prokhorov; front cover (inset) Rhode Island School of Design; pp. 5, 41, 45, 59, 64 © Autodesk; p. 7 Science & Society Picture Library/Getty Images; p. 9 © Walt Disney Pictures/courtesy Everett Collection; p. 11 © PRNewsFOTO/ Warner Bros. Consumer Products/AP Images; pp. 14, 52, 66 Center for Advanced Digital Applications – CADA/New York University/School of Continuing and Professional Studies; pp. 16, 22 © Bill Aron/PhotoEdit; p. 23 © Pixar-Disney/ Topham/The Image Works; p. 26 Murray Close/Moviepix/ Getty Images; p. 29 Johannes Eisele/AFP/Getty Images; p. 33 Courtesy Maxon Computer GmbH; p. 36 New Line/Photofest; pp. 39, 56 Gears of War® and Unreal Engine® 3 images used with permission. © 2013, Epic Games, Inc.; p. 47 Fotosearch Value/Getty Images; p. 50 Hill Street Studios/Blend Images/ Getty Images; p. 62 Buena Vista/Photofest; interior page border image © iStockphoto.com/Daniel Brunner, pp. 10, 21, 27, 34, 42, 55, 60, 65 (text box background) © iStockphoto .com/Nicholas Belton

Designer: Matthew Cauli; Photo Researcher: Marty Levick